£9.99

# Instant Art for

# CHRISTIANITY

## in R.E.

Key Stage 1

Illustrated by Debbie Clark

Compiled by Pete and Ruth Townsend

Kevin Mayhew

First published in 1997 in Great Britain by
KEVIN MAYHEW LTD
Rattlesden
Bury St Edmunds
Suffolk IP30 0SZ

ISBN  1 84003 092 5
Catalogue No  1396053

0 1 2 3 4 5 6 7 8 9


Cover and illustrations by Debbie Clark
Printed in Great Britain

# Contents

**Expression of Belief**

1   Spidergram

2   Symbols – cross, fish, crucifix, kneeling, bowing heads, hands together

3   Artefacts and Actions that Belong to Ceremonies – rings, font, candles, cross, bread, wine

**Feelings**

1   Spidergram

2-3   Illustrations of Feelings – awe, wonder, fear, sadness, pleasure, pride, security, loneliness, jealousy, love, elation, concern, admiration

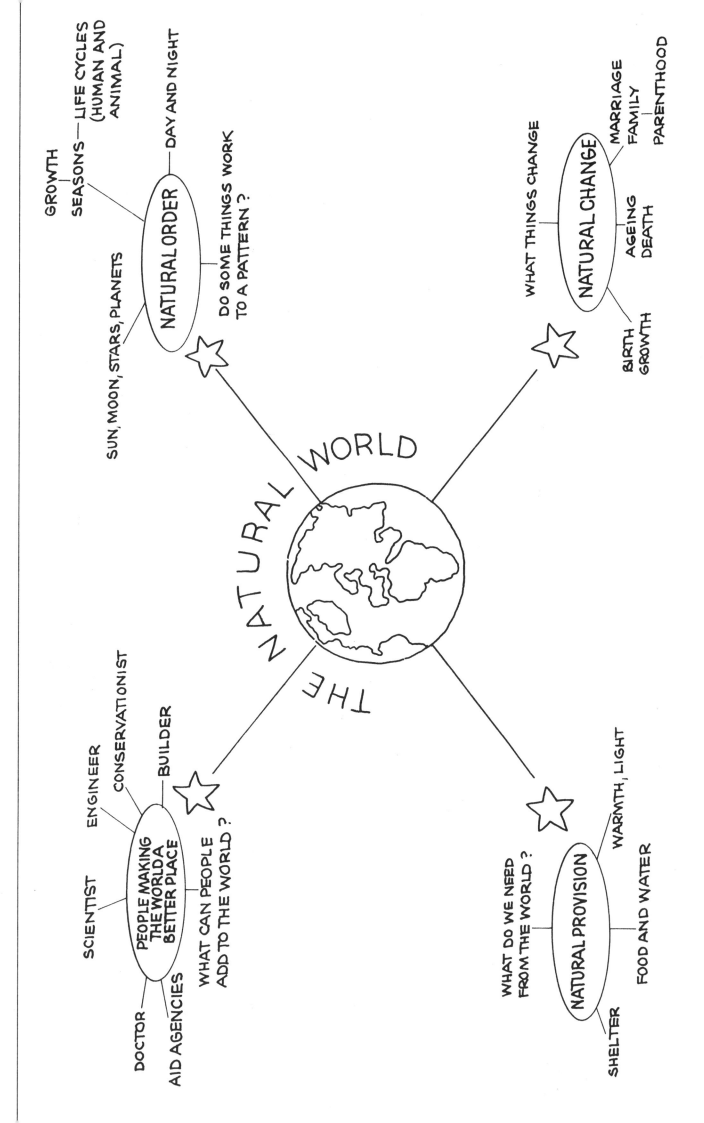

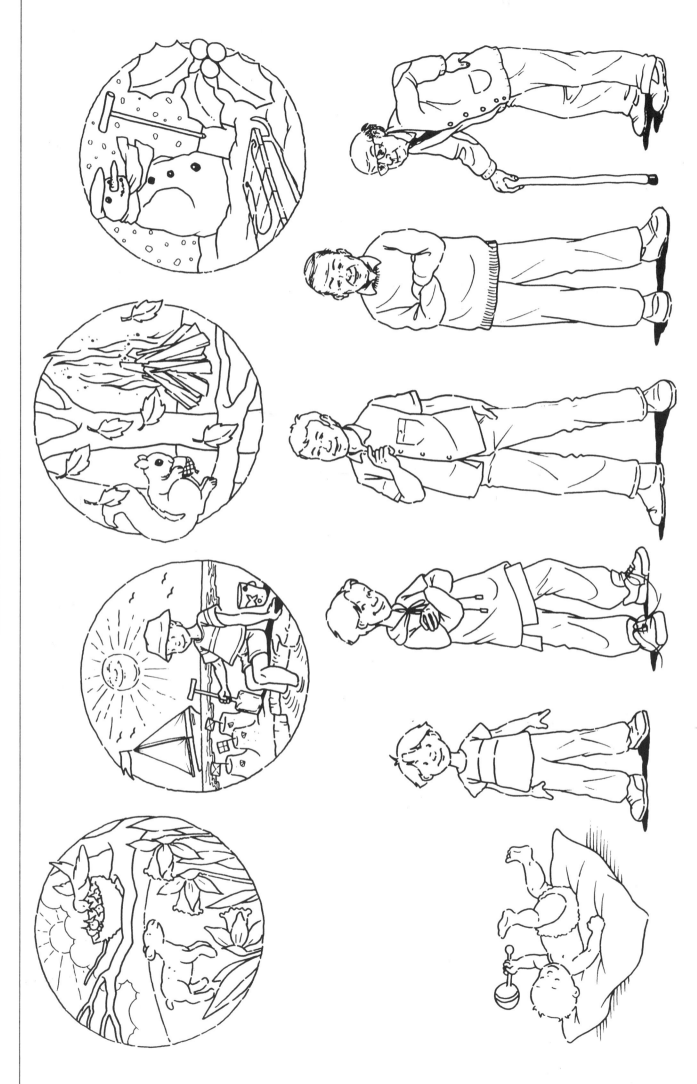

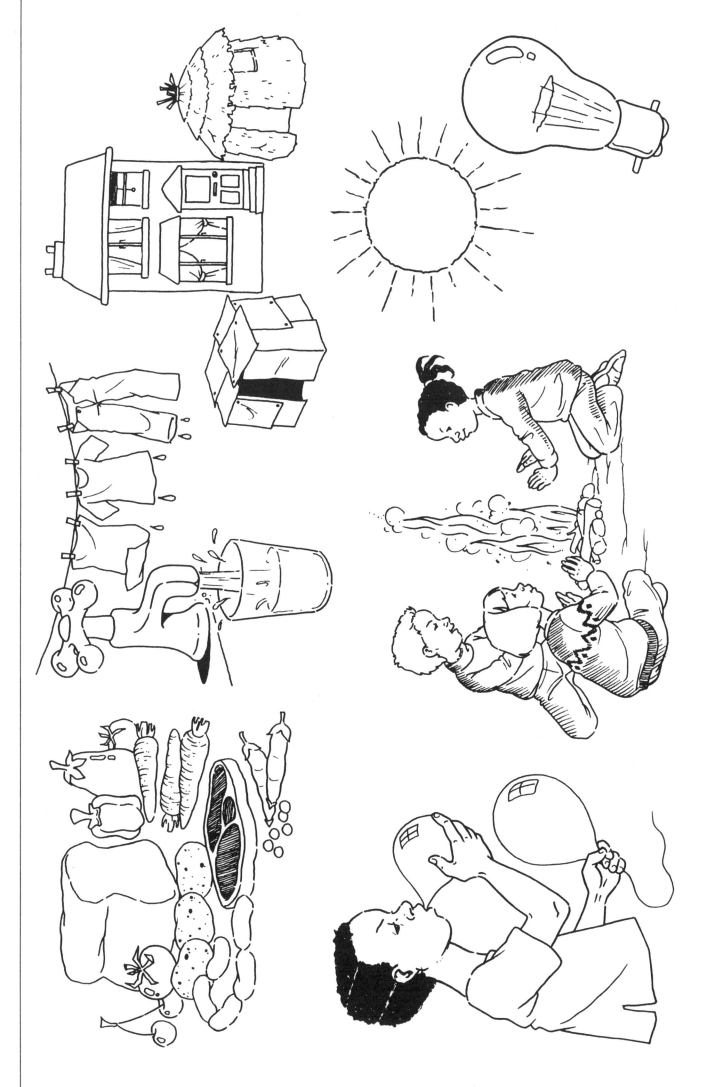

HUMAN RELATIONSHIPS

**Groups**
- FAMILY
- CLUBS
- FAITH GROUPS
- FRIENDS
- INTEREST GROUPS
- WHICH GROUP DO I BELONG TO?

**Individuals**
- IS EVERYBODY SPECIAL?
- DIFFERENCES
- TALENTS
- ACHIEVEMENTS
- DIFFERENT BACKGROUND

**Caring Actions**
- WHAT DO I CARE ABOUT?
- CARNIVAL
- COMMUNITY
- SCHOOL
- HOME

**Changing Relationships**
- BREAKING FRIENDS
- CHANGING SCHOOL
- MOVING HOUSE
- SAYING GOODBYE
- BEREAVEMENT
- WHY DO SOME THINGS HAVE TO CHANGE?

**What can I share?**
- MONEY
- FOOD
- PROMISES
- SMILES
- SECRETS
- TRUST
- LOVE
- FRIENDSHIP

**Caring People**
- WHO CARES ABOUT ME?
- PARENTS/FAMILY
- NURSE
- CROSSING WARDEN
- TEACHER
- POLICE OFFICER
- FIREFIGHTER

**Worldwide Relationships**
- WHO CARES FOR OTHERS?
- OXFAM
- SAVE THE CHILDREN
- CHILDLINE
- TRAIDCRAFT
- TEAR FUND
- W.W.F.

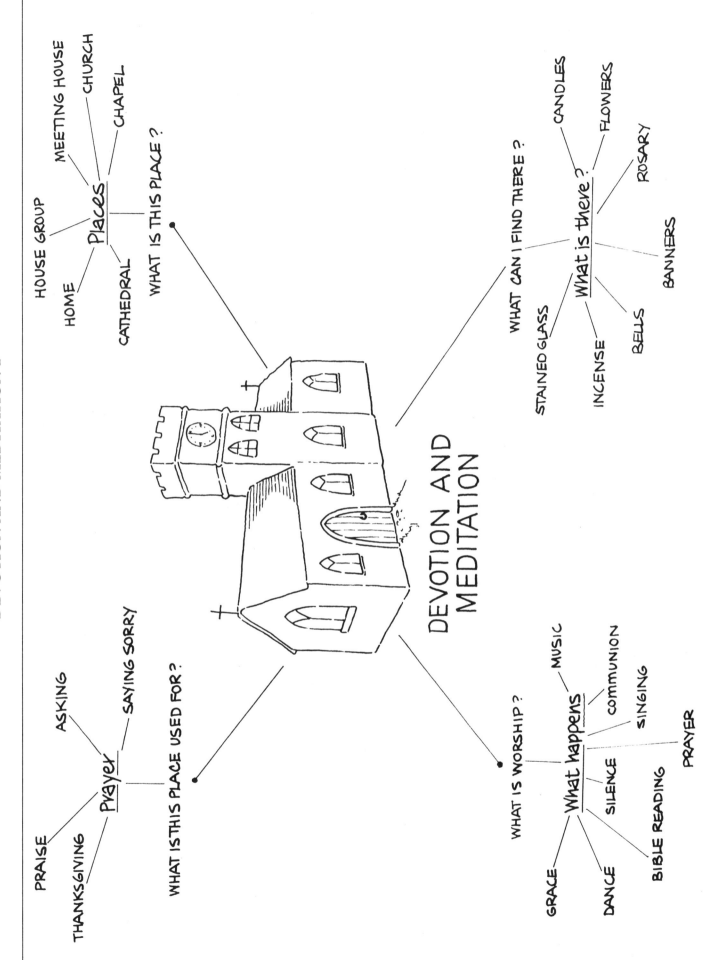

**Places** — WHAT IS THIS PLACE?
- MEETING HOUSE
- CHURCH
- CHAPEL
- HOUSE GROUP
- HOME
- CATHEDRAL

**What is there?** — WHAT CAN I FIND THERE?
- CANDLES
- FLOWERS
- ROSARY
- BANNERS
- BELLS
- INCENSE
- STAINED GLASS

**Prayer** — WHAT IS THIS PLACE USED FOR?
- ASKING
- SAYING SORRY
- PRAISE
- THANKSGIVING

DEVOTION AND MEDITATION

**What happens** — WHAT IS WORSHIP?
- MUSIC
- COMMUNION
- SINGING
- PRAYER
- BIBLE READING
- SILENCE
- DANCE
- GRACE

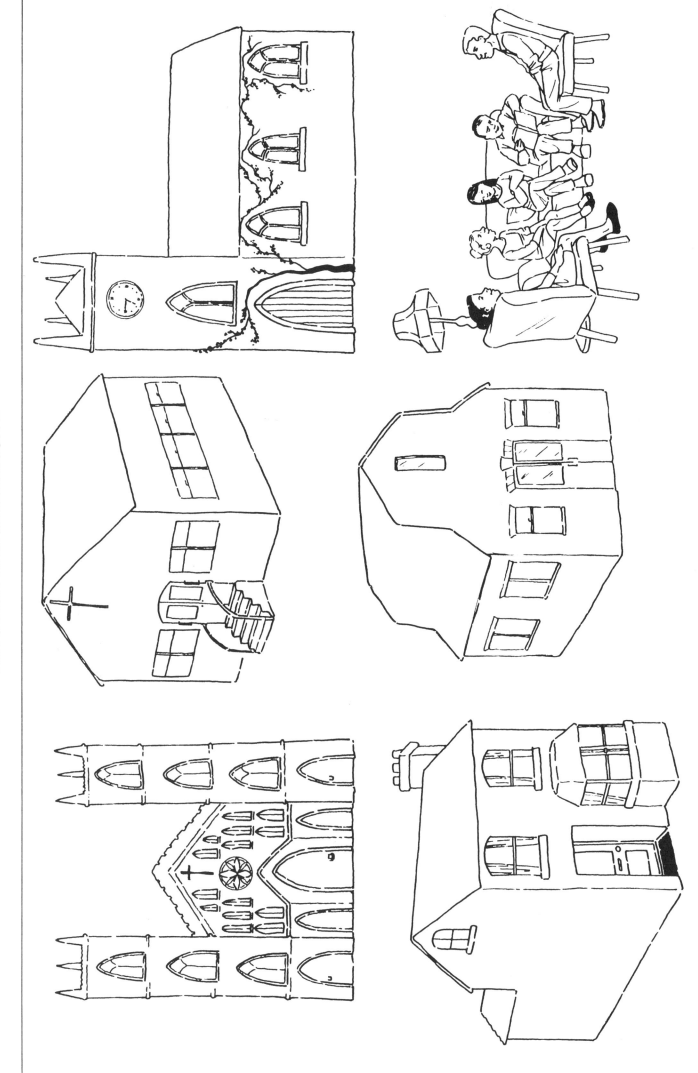

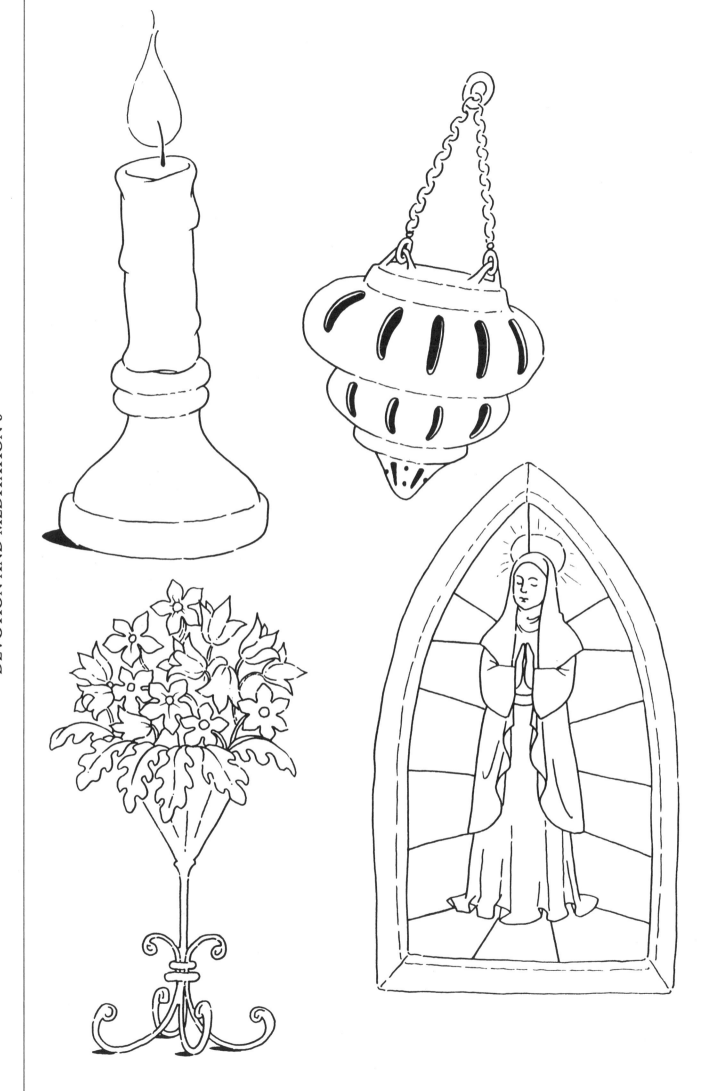

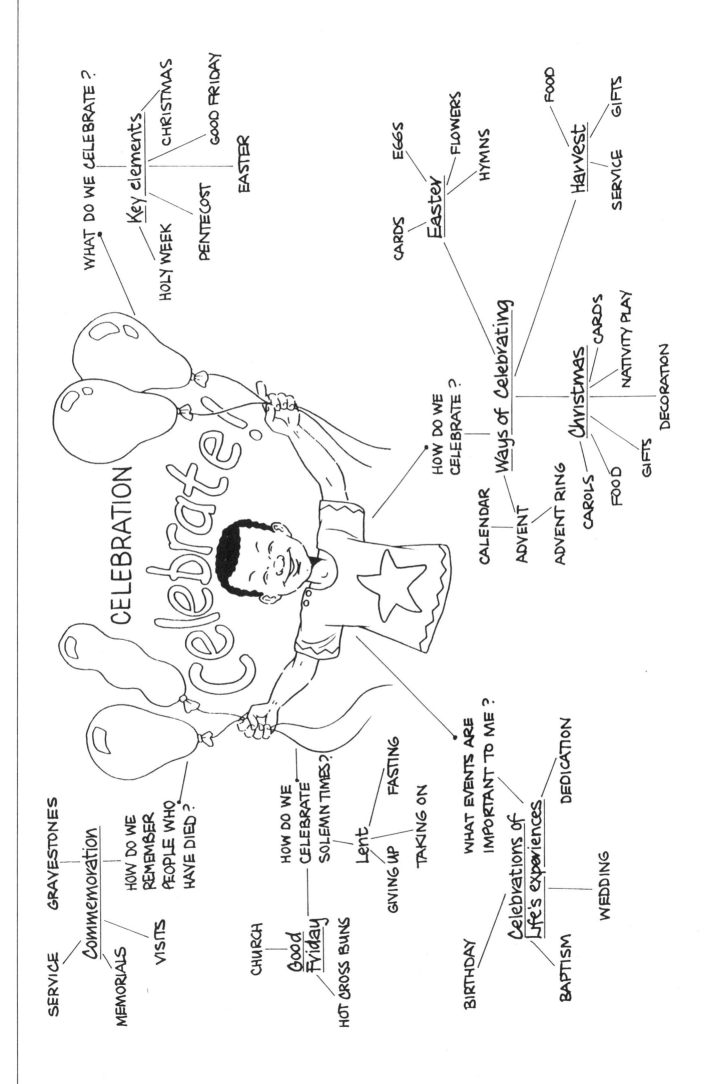

CELEBRATION

WHAT DO WE CELEBRATE?

Key elements
- CHRISTMAS
- GOOD FRIDAY
- EASTER
- PENTECOST
- HOLY WEEK

Easter
- EGGS
- FLOWERS
- HYMNS
- CARDS

Harvest
- FOOD
- GIFTS
- SERVICE

HOW DO WE CELEBRATE?

Ways of Celebrating

Christmas
- CARDS
- NATIVITY PLAY
- DECORATION
- GIFTS
- FOOD
- CAROLS

Advent
- CALENDAR
- ADVENT RING

Commemoration
HOW DO WE REMEMBER PEOPLE WHO HAVE DIED?
- SERVICE
- GRAVESTONES
- MEMORIALS
- VISITS

HOW DO WE CELEBRATE SOLEMN TIMES?

Good Friday
- CHURCH
- HOT CROSS BUNS

Lent
- FASTING
- TAKING ON
- GIVING UP

WHAT EVENTS ARE IMPORTANT TO ME?

Celebrations of Life's experiences
- DEDICATION
- WEDDING
- BAPTISM
- BIRTHDAY

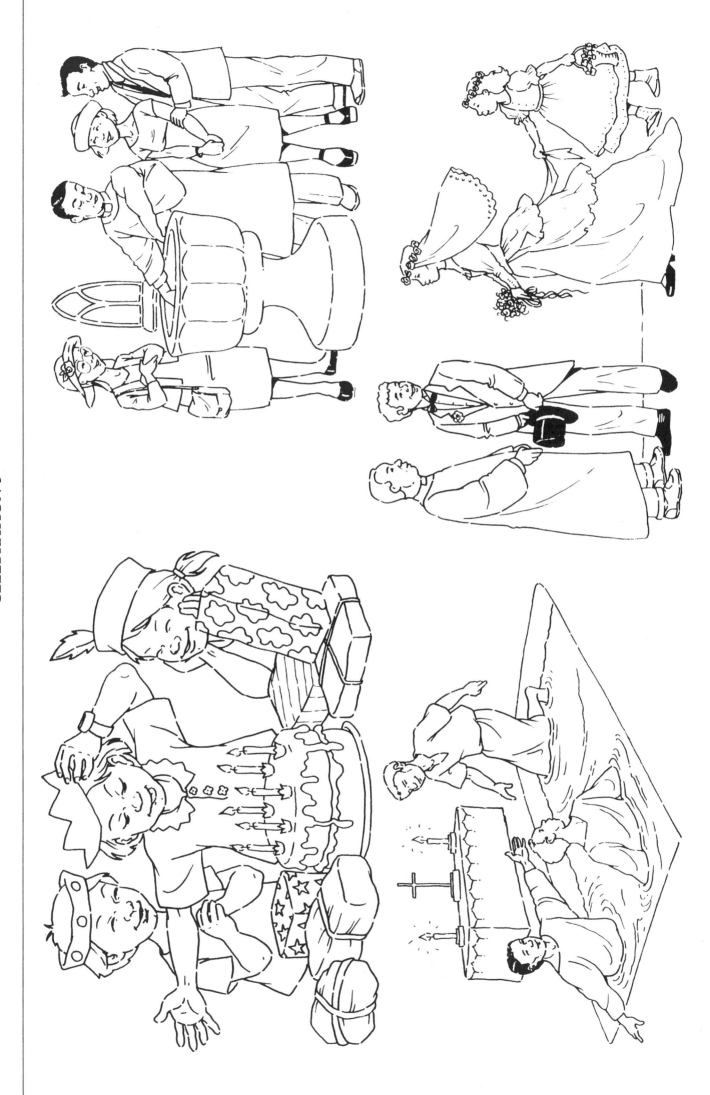

CELEBRATION 5

LIFESTYLE 1

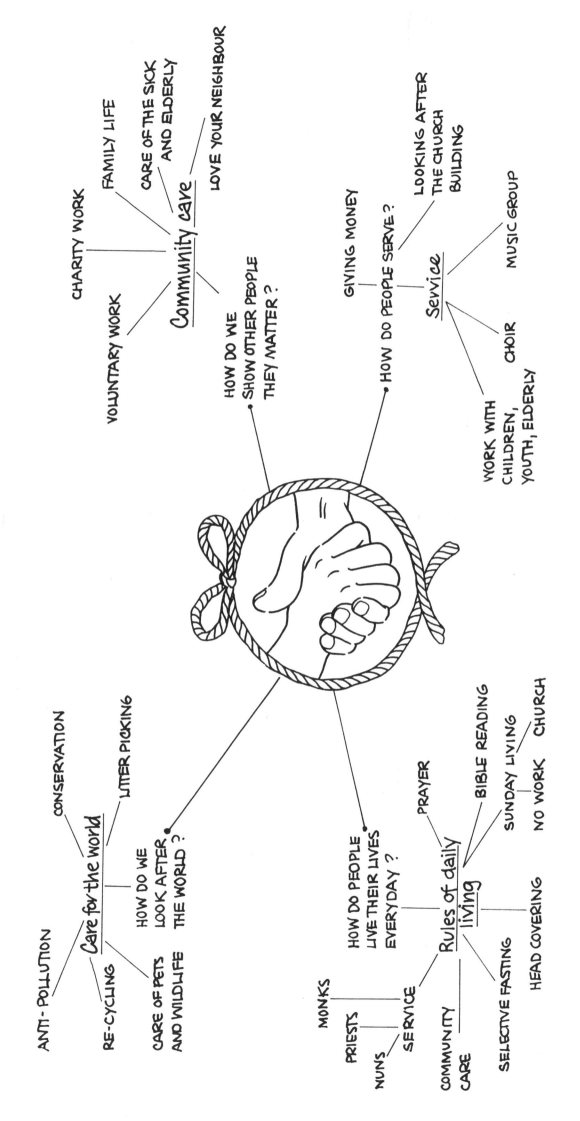

**Community care**
- CHARITY WORK
- FAMILY LIFE
- CARE OF THE SICK AND ELDERLY
- LOVE YOUR NEIGHBOUR
- VOLUNTARY WORK

HOW DO WE SHOW OTHER PEOPLE THEY MATTER?

**Service**
- GIVING MONEY
- LOOKING AFTER THE CHURCH BUILDING
- MUSIC GROUP
- CHOIR
- WORK WITH CHILDREN, YOUTH, ELDERLY

HOW DO PEOPLE SERVE?

**Care for the world**
- ANTI-POLLUTION
- CONSERVATION
- RE-CYCLING
- LITTER PICKING
- CARE OF PETS AND WILDLIFE

HOW DO WE LOOK AFTER THE WORLD?

**Rules of daily living**
- PRAYER
- BIBLE READING
- SUNDAY LIVING
- NO WORK
- CHURCH
- MONKS
- PRIESTS
- NUNS
- SERVICE
- COMMUNITY CARE
- SELECTIVE FASTING
- HEAD COVERING

HOW DO PEOPLE LIVE THEIR LIVES EVERYDAY?

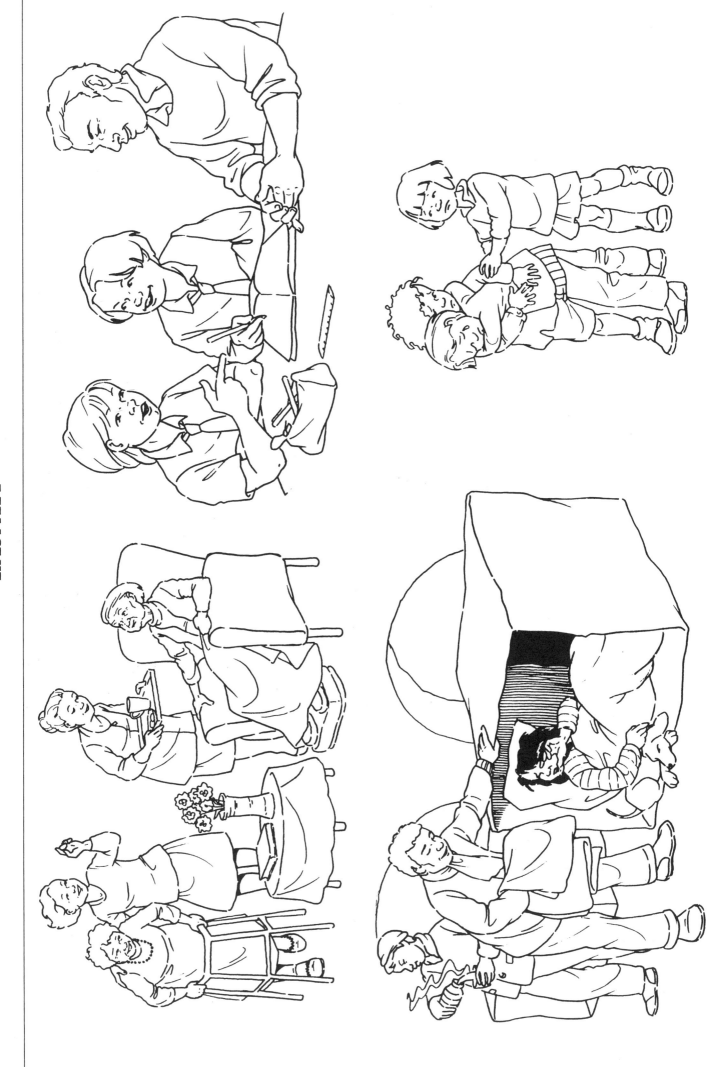

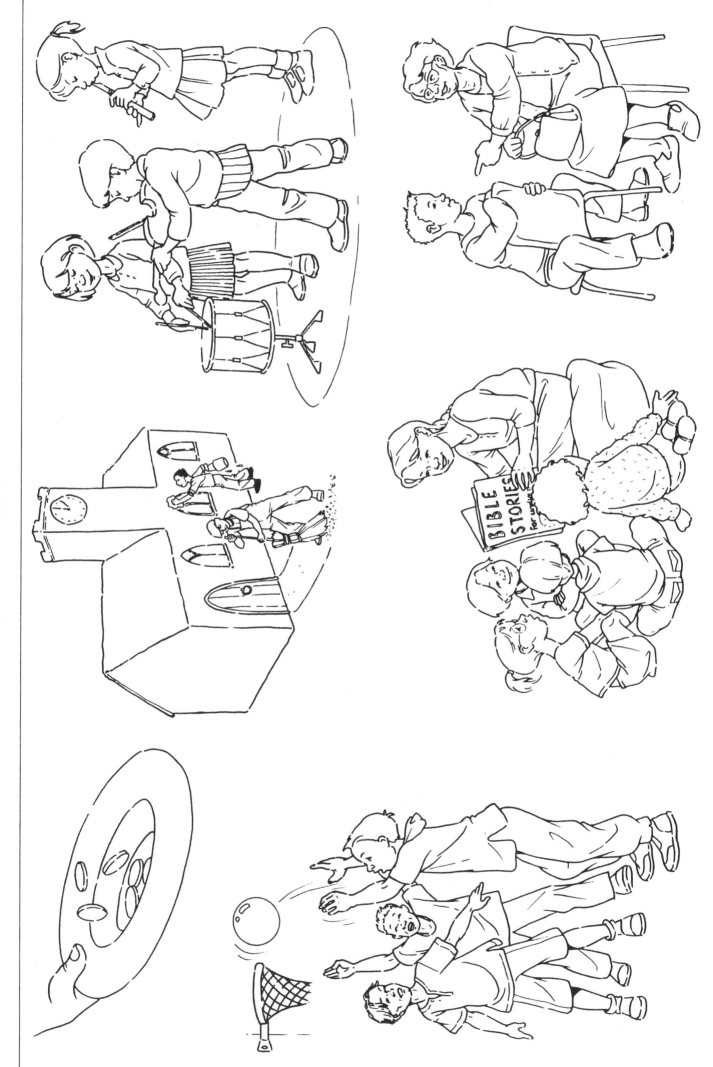

LIFESTYLE 4

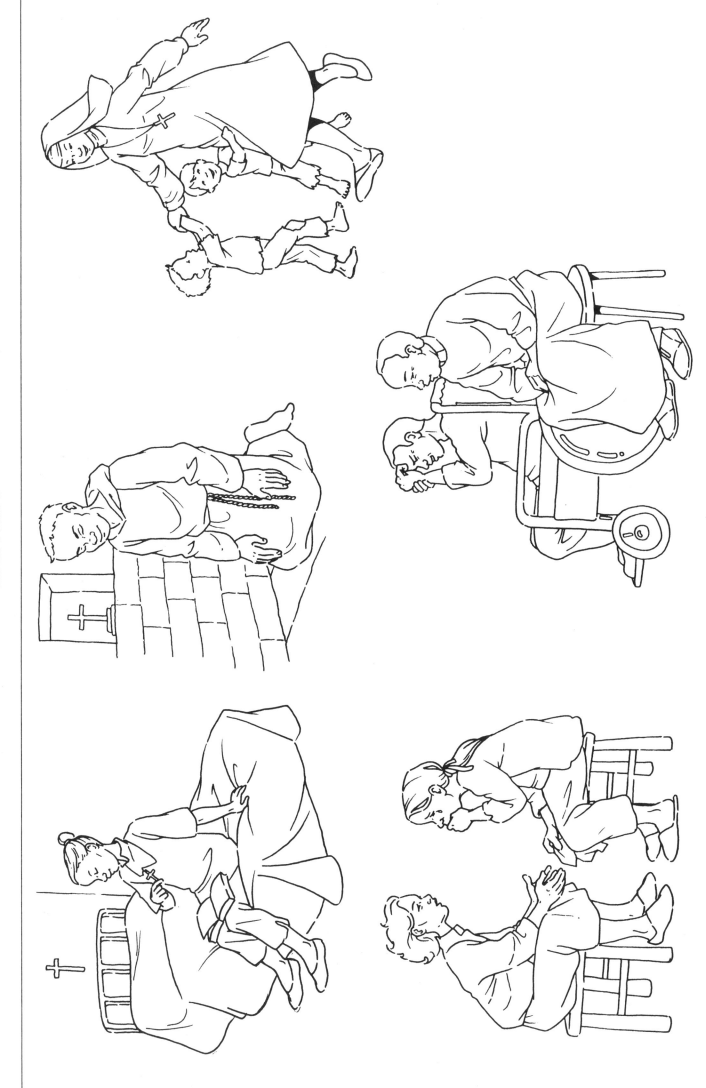

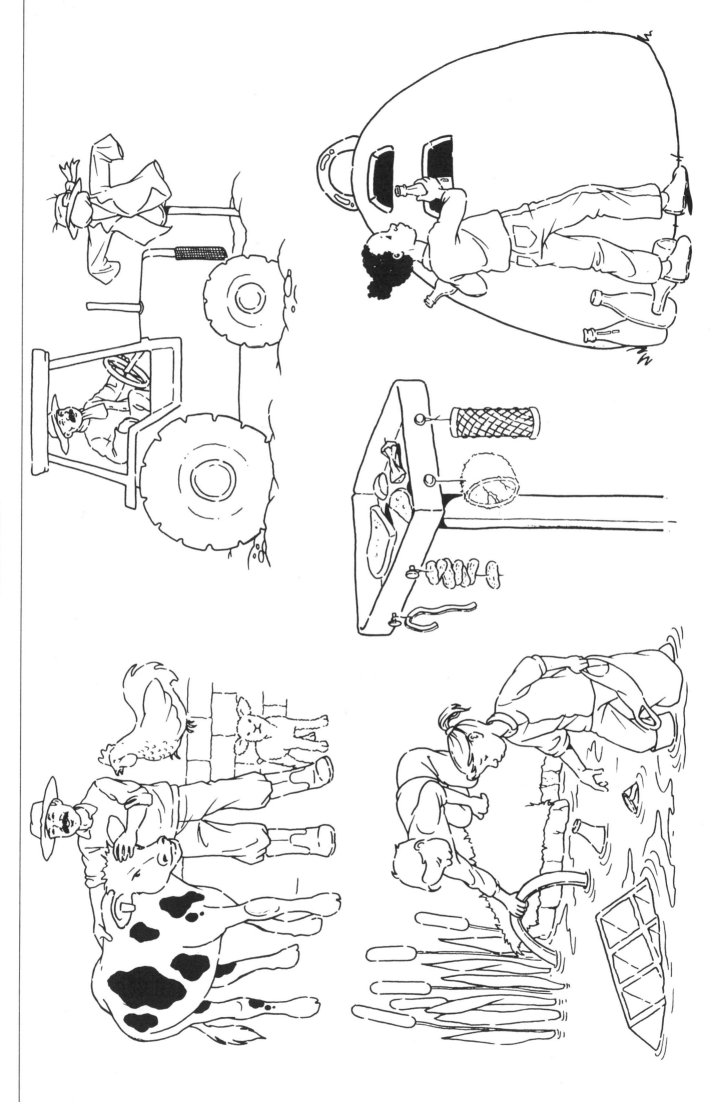

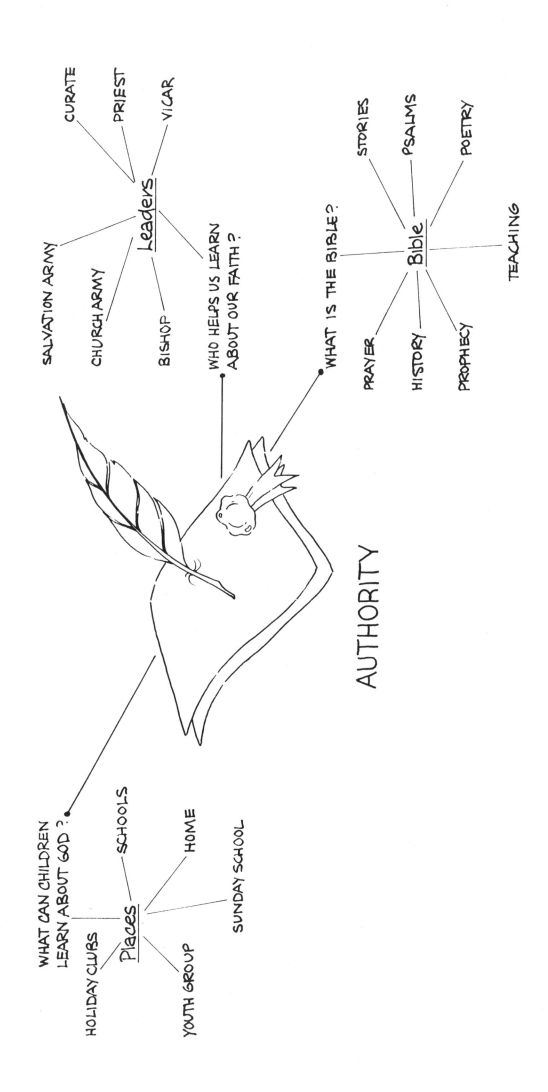

AUTHORITY

**Leaders**
- CURATE
- PRIEST
- VICAR
- SALVATION ARMY
- CHURCH ARMY
- BISHOP

WHO HELPS US LEARN ABOUT OUR FAITH?

**Bible**
- STORIES
- PSALMS
- POETRY
- TEACHING
- PROPHECY
- HISTORY
- PRAYER

WHAT IS THE BIBLE?

WHAT CAN CHILDREN LEARN ABOUT GOD?

**Places**
- SCHOOLS
- HOME
- SUNDAY SCHOOL
- YOUTH GROUP
- HOLIDAY CLUBS

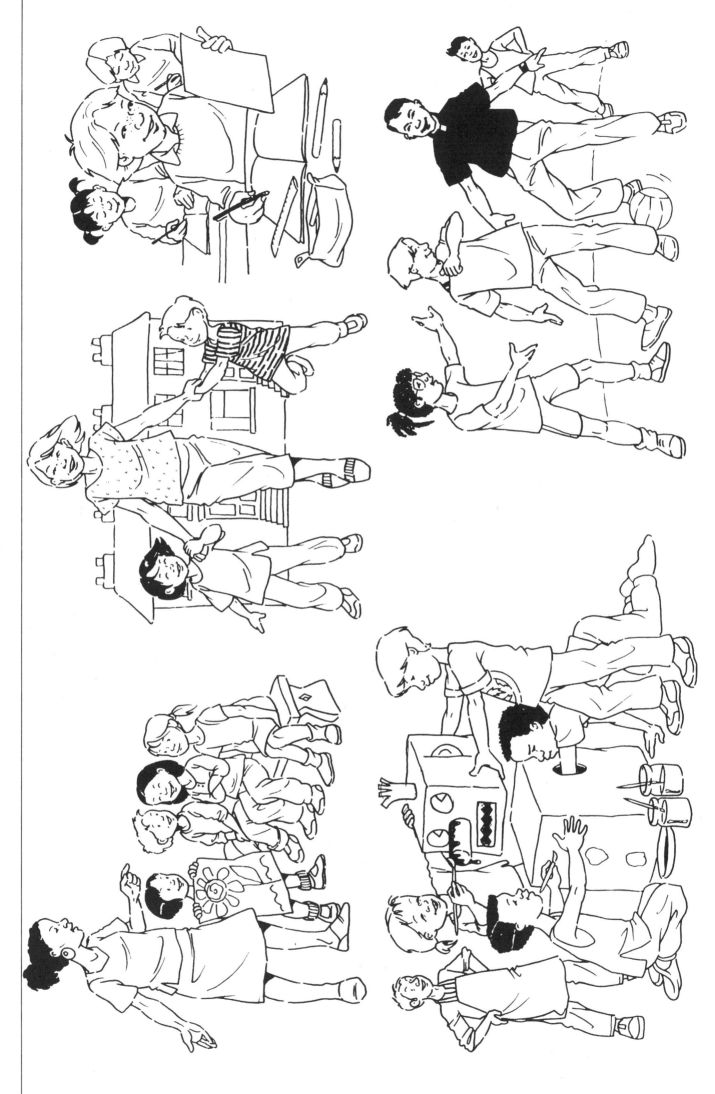

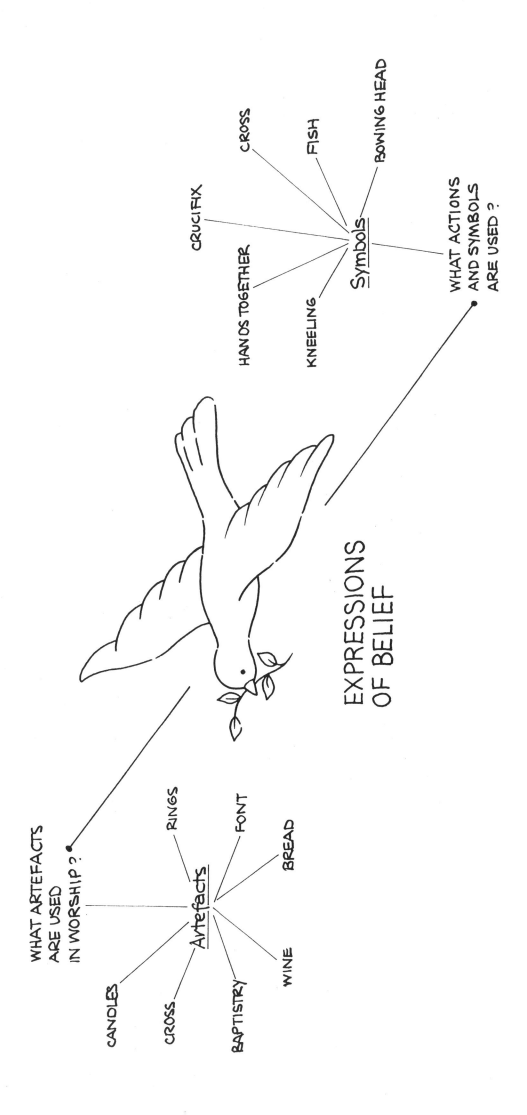

EXPRESSIONS
OF BELIEF

WHAT ACTIONS
AND SYMBOLS
ARE USED ?

Symbols
- CROSS
- FISH
- BOWING HEAD
- CRUCIFIX
- HANDS TOGETHER
- KNEELING

WHAT ARTEFACTS
ARE USED
IN WORSHIP ?

Artefacts
- RINGS
- FONT
- BREAD
- WINE
- BAPTISTRY
- CROSS
- CANDLES

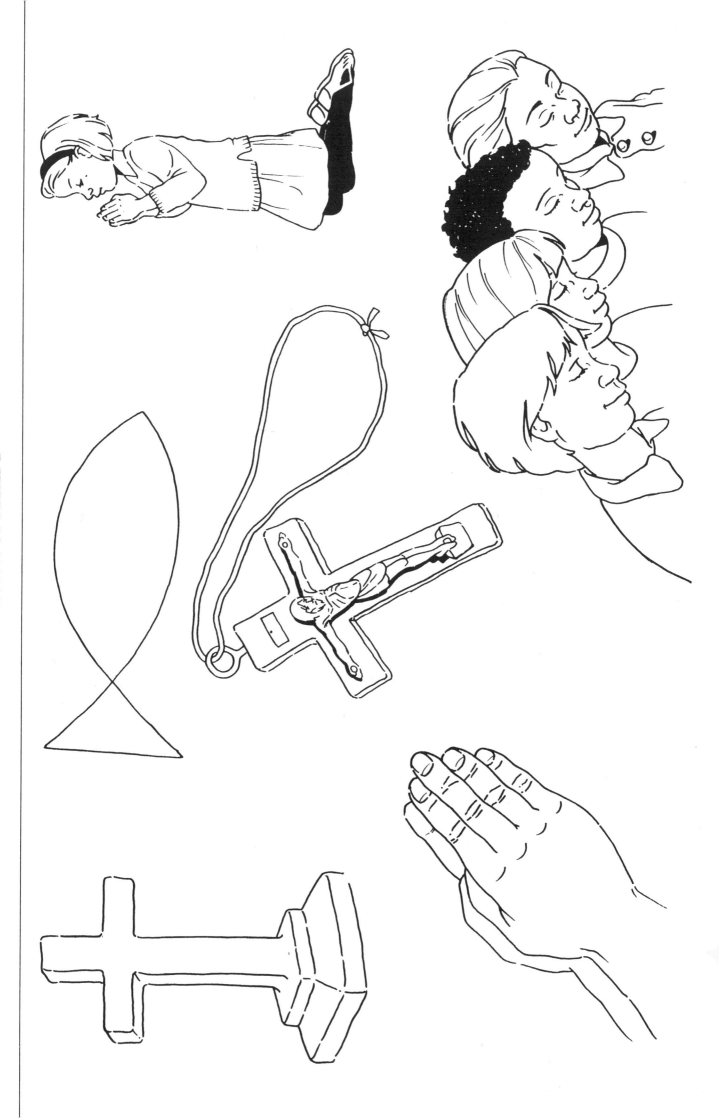

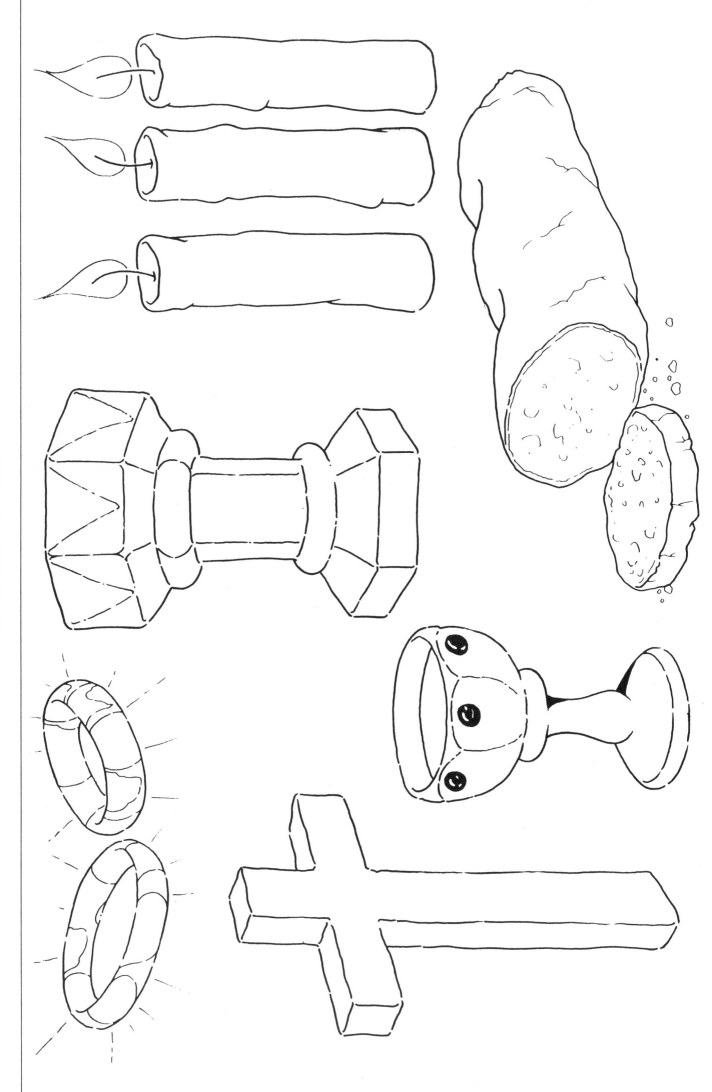

FEELINGS 1

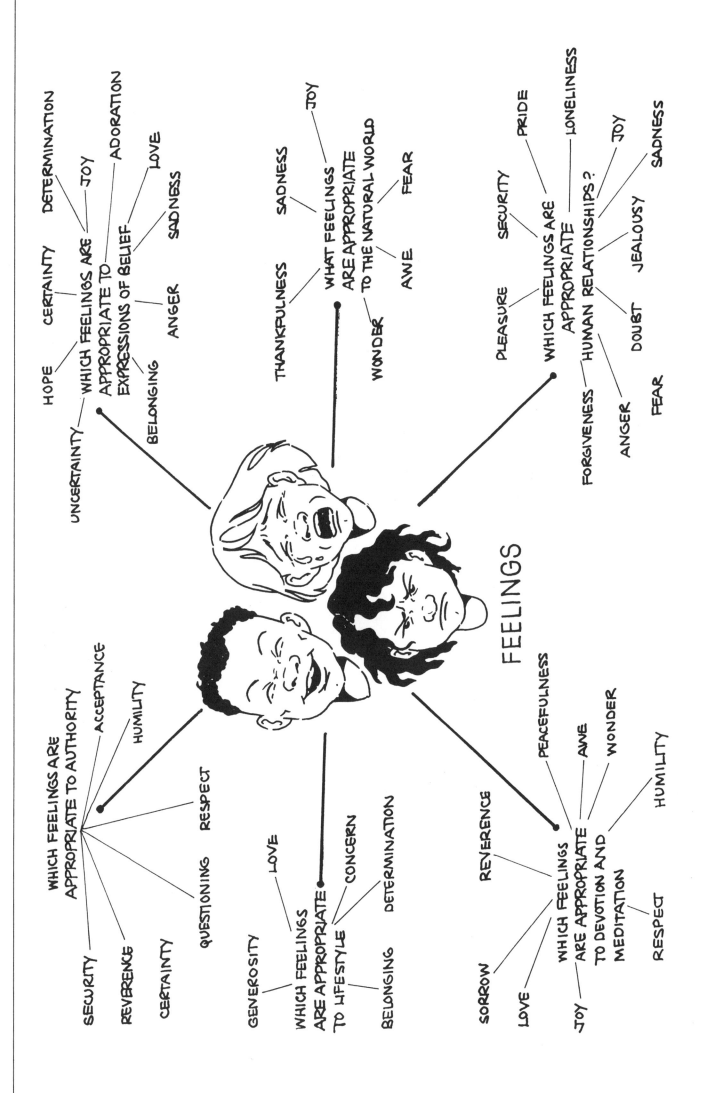

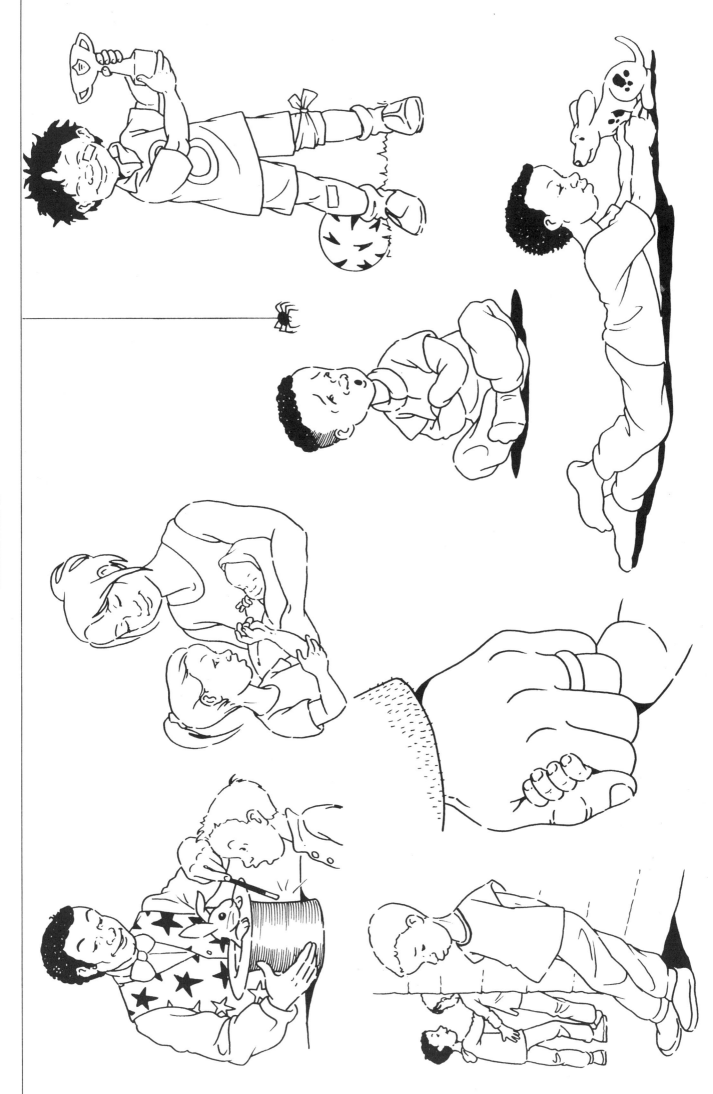

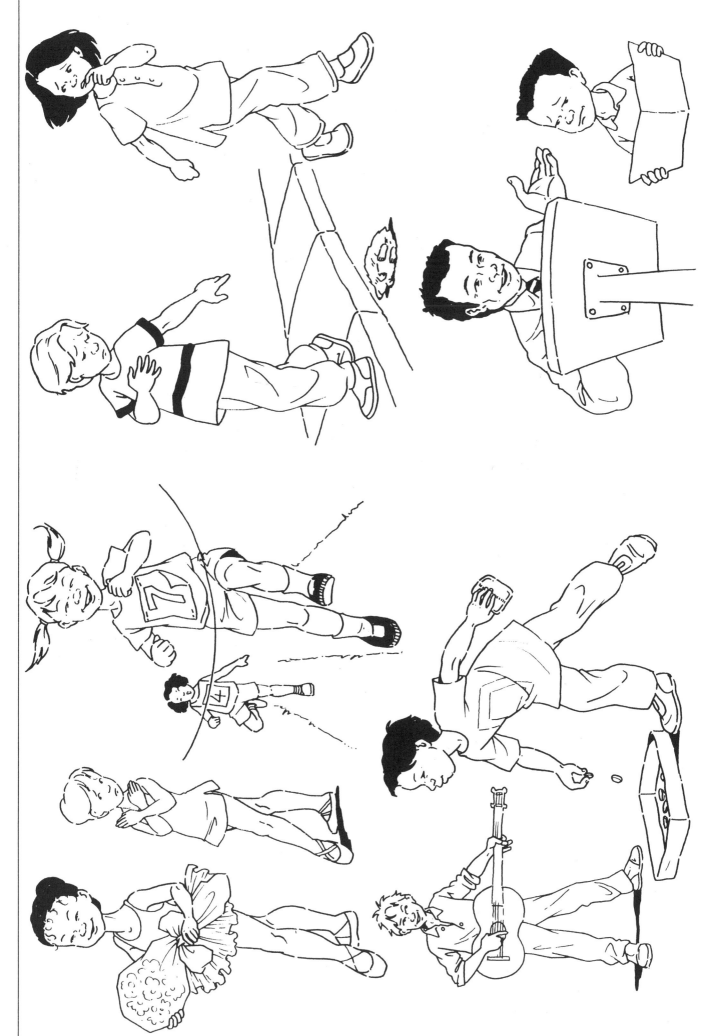